NOTE TO PARENTS

Welcome to Kingfisher Readers! This program is designed to help young readers build skills, confidence, and a love of reading as they explore their favorite topics.

These tips can help you get more from the experience of reading books together. But remember, the most important thing is to make reading fun!

Tips to Warm Up Before Reading

- Look through the book with your child. Ask them what they notice about the pictures.
- Wonder aloud together. Ask questions and make predictions. What will this book be about? What are some words we could expect to find on these pages?

While Reading

- Take turns or read together until your child takes over.
- Point to the words as you say them.
- When your child gets stuck on a word, ask if the picture could help. Then think about the first letter too.
- Accept and praise your child's contributions.

After Reading

- Look back at the things your child found interesting. Encourage connections to other things you both know.
- Draw pictures or make models to explore these ideas.
- Read the book again soon, to build fluency.

With five distinct levels and a wealth of appealing topics, the Kingfisher Readers series provides children with an exciting way to learn to read about the world around them. Enjoy!

Ellie Costa, M.S. Ed.
Literacy Specialist, Bank Street School for Children, New York

KINGFISHER
READERS

level
2

Fur and Feathers

Claire Llewellyn and
Thea Feldman

KINGFISHER
NEW YORK

KINGFISHER
LONDON & NEW YORK

Copyright © Kingfisher 2013
Published in the United States by Kingfisher,
175 Fifth Ave., New York, NY 10010
Kingfisher is an imprint of Macmillan Children's Books, London.
All rights reserved.

Distributed in the U.S. and Canada by Macmillan,
175 Fifth Ave., New York, NY 10010

Library of Congress Cataloging-in-Publication data
has been applied for.

Series editor: Thea Feldman
Literacy consultant: Ellie Costa, Bank Street College, New York

ISBN: 978-0-7534-7088-6 (HB)
ISBN: 978-0-7534-7089-3 (PB)

Kingfisher books are available for special promotions
and premiums. For details contact: Special Markets
Department, Macmillan, 175 Fifth Ave., New York, NY 10010.

For more information, please visit
www.kingfisherbooks.com

Printed in China
9 8 7 6 5 4 3 2 1
1TR/0713/WKT/UG/105MA

Picture credits
The Publisher would like to thank the following for permission to reproduce their material. Every care has
been taken to trace copyright holders. However, if there have been unintentional omissions or failure to trace
copyright holders, we apologize and will, if informed, endeavor to make corrections in any future edition.
Top = t; Bottom = b; Center = c; Left = l; Right = r
Cover Shutterstock/Richard Peterson; Pages 4 Shutterstock/Michael Pettigrew; 5t Shutterstock/Jeffrey
Van Daele; 5b Shutterstock/holbox; 6 Shutterstock/iDesign; 7t Shutterstock/FloridaStock;
7b Shutterstock/Studio 37; 8 Alamy/Wayne Hutchinson; 9 Photolibrary/OSF; 10–11 Photolibrary/Alaska
Stock; 11 Photolibrary/OSF; 12 Photolibrary/F1 online; 13 Photolibrary/Alaska Stock; 14 Frank Lane
Picture Agency (FLPA)/Mitsuaki Iwago/Minden; 15 Photolibrary/Bios; 16 Photolibrary/OSF; 17 FLPA/
Gerard Lacz; 18 Photolibrary/Bios; 19t Photolibrary/Animals Animals; 19b Photolibrary/Bios; 20 FLPA/B.
Borrrell Casals; 21t Photolibrary/OSF; 21b Photolibrary/Imagebroker; 22–23 Photolibrary/OSF;
24 Shutterstock/Eric Iselee; 25 Photolibrary/Peter Arnold; 26 FLPA/Konrad Wothe/Minden;
27 Photolibrary/Aflo Foto Agency; 28–29 Photolibrary/OSF; 29 Photolibrary/Imagebroker;
30 Shutterstock/Pavel Losevsky; 31t Shutterstock/Alexander Gitlits; 31b Photolibrary/Whitez.

Contents

Animals with fur

Some animals have hair.

Thick, soft hair is called fur.

Animals with hair or fur
are called **mammals**.

A sheep has thick, curly hair called wool.

You are a mammal too!

What kind of hair do you have?

Animals with feathers

Birds are animals with feathers.

Most birds have feathers all over their bodies.

A tiny hummingbird has about 900 feathers.

A bird has different kinds
of feathers.

Strong tail and wing feathers
help a bird fly.

Soft feathers
called **down** are
under the strong
feathers.

What fur and feathers do

Fur or feathers help an animal stay warm.

Fur or feathers stop
an animal's body heat
from escaping.

They keep cold air out too.

Keeping warm

When fur covers a mammal's body, it is called a **coat**.

A polar bear has a very warm coat, because it lives where it is cold.

The coat has long, thick top hairs that keep out the cold and wet.

Short, fluffy hairs underneath help keep the body's heat from escaping.

Keeping dry

Ducks and other birds that live in water have oil on their feathers.

This keeps water away from the skin.

Thick fur keeps water away from a sea otter's skin.

Cleaning fur

A mammal scratches or licks its coat to clean it.

This is called grooming.

Some animals groom each other.

Chimpanzees check each other's fur for dirt and pests like fleas.

Cleaning feathers

This bird is washing its feathers.

A bird also cleans its feathers
with its beak.

This is called preening.

Most birds lose their feathers
once a year.

Clean, new feathers grow in!

Growing fur

Some mammals, like hamsters, are born with no fur.

Baby hamsters stay together in their **nest** to keep warm.

A baby hamster starts to grow fur when it is five days old.

After two weeks a hamster has its full fur coat and can leave the nest.

Growing feathers

Some birds **hatch** without feathers.

These babies stay warm in their nest, just like hamsters.

They start to grow feathers when they are five days old.

After two weeks, the baby bird has all its feathers.

A sharp-looking coat!

A porcupine is a mammal that has hair on its body.

But it also has sharp spines that can grow almost 5 inches (13 centimeters) long!

Most of the time the spines lie flat.

A porcupine lifts its spines
when it thinks an animal is
going to attack.

Look at me!

A male peacock has bright tail feathers that he spreads out and shakes when he looks for a **mate**.

A male lion has a thick, furry **mane**.

A mane makes a lion look
big and strong and helps him
find a mate.

Hide and seek

Some animals' coats help them hide from **predators**.

The weasel blends in with plants and leaves on the ground and is hard to see.

An owl's feathers help it
blend in with the tree **bark**.

It sleeps hidden in plain sight!

Coats that change

The coats of some animals,
like this arctic fox,
change with the seasons!

In the winter, the coat is thick and white to keep the fox warm and help it blend in with the snow.

In the summer, the snow melts and the fox's coat turns brown.

A coat for you!

You have hair, but you still need help to stay warm and dry.

When it is cold,
you wear a coat.

You can wear warm hats, scarves, and gloves made from wool.

When it rains, you can put on a raincoat and boots!

Glossary

bark the outside of a tree trunk

coat fur or feathers that cover an animal's body

down small, soft, fluffy feathers

hatch to break out of an egg

mammal an animal with hair or fur that gives birth to its babies and feeds them milk

mane thick fur around the neck of an adult male lion

mate the partner that an animal has babies with

nest a place where an animal has babies and the babies stay warm and safe

predator an animal that hunts and eats other animals

If you have enjoyed reading
this book, look out for more in
the Kingfisher Readers series!

Collect
and read
them all!

KINGFISHER READERS: LEVEL 2

Fur and Feathers ☐
Trucks ☐
What Animals Eat ☐
Where Animals Live ☐
Where We Live ☐
Your Body ☐

KINGFISHER READERS: LEVEL 3

Ancient Rome ☐
Cars ☐
Creepy-Crawlies ☐
Dinosaur World ☐
Record Breakers—The Biggest ☐
Volcanoes ☐

For a full list of Kingfisher Readers books, plus
guidance for teachers and parents and activities
and fun stuff for kids, go to the Kingfisher Readers
website: **www.kingfisherreaders.com**